Cold Coffee at
Emo Court

Cold Coffee at Emo Court

Arthur Broomfield

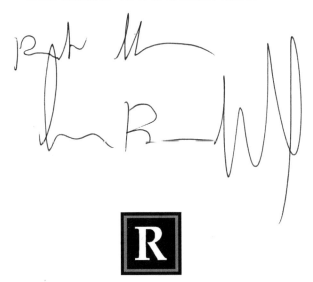

R

A REViVAL POETRY BOOK

Revival Press

Limerick - Ireland

Revival Press is the poetry imprint of
The Limerick Writers' Centre
12 Barrington Street, Limerick, Ireland

www.limerickwriterscentre.com
www.facebook.com/limerickwriterscentre

~

Book and Cover Design: Lotte bender
Managing Editor Revival Press: Dominic Taylor
Cover Image: Photograph by Arna Rúnarsdóttir, of Gunnuhver by Patricia Bennett.
Reproduced by kind permission of the artist.

ISBN 978-0-9934101-5-4

A CIP catalogue number for this publication is available from The British Library

We acknowledge the support of The Limerick Writers' Centre

For Assumpta

Acknowledgements

Acknowledgements are due to the editors of the following publications where some of these poems have been published *Acumen, Agenda, Crannog, Envoi, Cyphers, Honest Ulsterman, Icarus, Kim Moore's blog, Leinster Express, New Irish Writings Sunday Tribune, Ofi, Orbis, Outburst, Poetry Bus, Poetry Ireland Review, Salmon, Stony Thursday, The Galway Review, Tipperary Star, Writing North East, And Agamemnon Dead anthology, The Sea anthology, Envoi Summer Anthology 1990, From Here to the Horizon, Laois anthology 1999, Dundalk Patrick Kavanagh anthology.*

Very many thanks go to Mary O'Donnell and Jean O'Brien for their critical readings of these poems, without you this book would not have been possible.

CONTENTS

'What is natural to mankind is not spoken language but the faculty of constructing a language.'

— Jean-Jacques Rousseau

Portlaoise at 46

Coffee in Jim's Country Kitchen
or The Regency with friends.
An exchange rate is striking here
each transaction
a hieroglyphic
etched on a milestone
paving my journey home.

This place knows my value
my roots are beneath it.
Here my growth has been organic.

So when someone smiles
in recognition
or beams a hard currency
'how's it going'?
I glow,
well,
legal tender.

The Bridge Club 1916
After a tapestery

She can calm the crater
in the pit of her stomach
with trays of éclairs
and chocolate fudge
for the church bazaar

and sedate the wounds
on her strawberry flan
with soft breaths
of her cream and pastry knife.

All cockades and corsets
and stiff upper lip
dreading a bad hand to south
like bad news from The Somme
she'll continue her game of bridge
Because it's expected of her.

Image of my Father

I was curled in a ball
on the leatherette couch,
quiescent in the July sun.

Someone on the BBC
was singing 'It's a good day'.

You were firm at the helm
of your armchair,
eyes fixed on some nautical star,
wearing your Lloyd George look
and believing *The Irish Times*.

Coming Home From Irey

My father in the front
of the child-full trap,
holding the whip he never used,
praising us home
from the summer palace
through the remote townlands
of Clondarrig and Ross.

And road-wise Charlie,
on the time-trapped track,
dressed up to kill
in his harness of black,
wrote his steps in the felt-soft pad
that hid the half-blind potholes
from each other's view.

How secure we were
in the confidence of a dust wrap,
coddled together on the down-soft seat
of the spring-live trap;
feasting on a nectar
of furze and heather scent
and a theophany of summer twilight,
or once, in a rising moon,
being anointed with the magic
of a falling dewdrop.

And I pondering
the dichotomous cowslip
my father told me
only grew in poor land.

The Night Bannan's Threshing Mill Arrived in our Yard
In memory of Johnny Bannan who died May 11 2011

Johnny Bannan won my respect
the day he declined to wash his hands
'they're grand Ma'am, thanks';
he spoke with the assurance
of one who knows his options.
My mother fussed
and poured his tea.

His overalls, decorated
with medals of exotic grease
sparkled in the reflection
of the Aladdin lamp
that lit our kitchen.
Amorphous transfers
to his face and neck,
from his oily fingers,
confirmed the mystical status
of the Lieutenant of the Leviathan.

I imagined his railwayman's cap
badged and braided,
the armour plated engine storming along the front,
he leaning out the side door
barking glad tidings
of bushel weight
to expectant farmers,
at agricultural speed.

I, held back on my father's knee,
wanted to be second in command
in his benevolent army,
to be there when he swung
the starting handle that fired the pistons,
to carry the drums of T.V.O.
that smelled of the future,
to befriend him,
to give him a hand.

The Poetry Reading at Semple Stadium

The first poetry reading
I ever attended
was at Semple Stadium
in the early days
of my love affair
with Tipperary.

Everyone else thought
it was a hurling match
but I knew it was a reading
when I heard the poet
rhapsodise the names
Of GAA clubs
through the charged aura
of a hurling stadium
from his bunker
beneath the New Stand.

Isolated on his podium
by ticket sellers
counting out their takings
the Ezra Pound of Thurles
shocked me with the excitement
of the spoken word.

As he read out the names
Carrick-Davins, Lorrha,
Boherlahan-Dualla,
Moycarkey, Roscrea,
Kilruane-McDonagh
and Borrisoleigh.
the fans cheered their players
and their clubs.

And I cheered the poet
for giving me back
my love of language.

The Manchester United Crash at Munich
February 6th 1958

You were ironing clothes
when I came in from school
the iron heavy with intent
driving to the tip of the board
each crease-seeking stroke
smoothing and warming
and shaping
the sleeves and collar
of my good shirt.

There were some survivors.

"Poor Matt Busby's in hospital"
you told me.

We shared the silences
between newsflashes
my eyes avoiding the dinner
I couldn't eat.

Your iron melting the ice
off the wings of the plane
at Munich.

Listening to the IRA through Italia '90

You have forced back the boundary
and added new words
to the language
Abercorn – Darkly – Ian Gow –
baggage to declare
at Cagliari and Palermo.

You've created space
and stretched meaning
as tight as barbed wire,
each nuance soaked in blood,
like the flag we were ashamed to wave
in Sicily.

We almost want to sing
ole, ole, ole
when you whinge
about Gibralter and Loughgall.

Sick of what we're becoming
we long for that post-revolutionary dullness:
you're on some podium
having lapsed into the half-truths
of political respectability,
your chest puffed with medals
berating the guilty bystanders.

A lost motorist, an Italian tourist, perhaps,
will inquire the way to Enniskillen

The Return of Mairéad Farrell

You are home now,
In death the adequate heroine.
A warrior queen
above absolution,
riding in pride,
Boadicea, on your chariot.

A Catholic Country

She had been,
Mrs Moore made it known,
out late with a fella,
the girl who'd been hustled to hospital
battered black and blue
by her father.

My mother
who was a Protestant
listened. It wasn't the done thing
to protest when matters sensitive
to the other side showed up..

Her mother, said Mrs Moore,
was with the girl close to her bed.

She was in a terrible state.

The Sisters of Mercy who ran
the hospital and doing his rounds,
the priest,
understood a family matter.

The Divorce Referendum 1986

You had taken up
a special position
at the farthest end
of the convent railing,
your back turned
to the voters, like a man
who was wrestling
with an informed conscience
and losing.

At least you were there –
for the last half hour –
you can always say
'I was at the funeral'.

And your face
your face,
I wanted to give you a *Rennie.*
You knew something I hadn't been told,
Didn't you ?

Did your gay lover
Threaten to tell your wife?

Safer the cosy mucus
of mother churches anus.

On the Way for my Vasectomy

On the way for my vasectomy
I passed a signpost
to Kilcock.
Haunted by the omen
I mentioned it to Dr Rynne.

My friends still ask me
does it hurt,
do you miss any thing,
does it feel the same?

Well, I sometimes tell them,
I was on that road again, lately
And the signpost is still there.

Some days when you meet another like

the day I met
Charles McPherson
I said are you Charles McPherson?
He said yes I am, or something like that,
in Cork,
in the rain.

I said I'm going to your concert
and gripped his hand tight
with my two hands.
Not having met Beethoven
I didn't want to let it go.

Durrow County Laois

At times I get close
to what made me.
So close I could say
this is it
this is the moment

that eventually slips out of focus

in Durrow, County Laois
an old photograph hangs
in the Copper Kettle coffee shop,
fired up faces
at a Home Rule rally.
All that peasant passion
embarrasses.

Fly Thoughts on Golden Wings 2

In respect of bald Garibaldi's
suspects in italics
do nation
undone
Donatella

Verdi Monteverdi Monte Cassino
mangled Mussolini
hanging in the air
the food of love

Otto Skorzeny
the roaming Roman
singing in the reign
fly over the cock cuckoo's nest
goose-stepping merrily on high.

A stab
at mater
Joyce mad sad an' had
rejoiced

the Pa-
trick
Alive alive o
a live alive o
cock-
els muscles
a live a
li-va – oh.

Eqinox

A gap declares itself,
against the odds
where mist and mountains merge,
dims the awe of seasons.

Corn stack clouds
float off the fecund earth,
meadowsweet and ghostly goat's - beard
renounce the corpus as the autumn equinox
spreads its ineffable charm
through the arc of the orb.

The firmament is becalmed,
sound a risk too great to squander,
defined light the ultimate tragedy.

If there is a time
to believe the void
it is now.
Today I will dare
to speak to the Gods.

Tokyo – Clonreher

Rush hour in the subway
in Tokyo Japan, they stomach
the sweat and stress of
humid July days,
mindful that towards evening
the Cicada will sing in the *min*
mi min min mi,
the fulfilled promise
that quiets and cools.

Axel squeaks, horse strains
in the incidental soil,
Danny forks from the dung draped cart,
sporadic heaps, my destiny to tease
The world to shape,
within the boundaries of a straight drill;

I work towards dinnertime
and dream of that top wedge
of the bog field
where the giant beech's
spring dress rustles the cicada's song.

Arrivals! Oohs and aahs
station guards tussle the tired
to griddle top trains.
I collapse, water to mouth,
Cicada in the purging beech,
blossoms in the undergrowth.

Beyond the Pain Barrier

'Never expose a thing of guilt and holy dread so great it appals the earth'.
- Sophocles

A thought – to write an epic
of paint peeling from a country pump,
of dusty roads and potholes chorused
in the tongue of the culture –
falls to the well of its language.

I want to begin at Omega,
when all is done and said,
when the last leaves of November
have deformed the barren earth,
when May mornings, Bach at Emo Court,
are no more than empty notes -
all that's left of names that meant
so much though it's Greek to even you,
at that end of time, time,
that's not time, that spell *it is broken* -

dissolving in the purity of night,
being the eye that sees nothing,
 the ear immune to lyre and truth,
to each iota of twisted opinion,

drawing from that which I cannot draw;
yet wonder was it blue then,
am I really well?

Emo Court

Cold coffee,
chipped porcelain
beside the out of tune piano
that played on,
the *Trompe l'oeil* in the foyer.

The lit candles we sketched
in the shadows
to subdue the blameless night

I view now from a separate table
across the liminal space.

A vapour wafts through,
a rusted key admits
an alto from the ethers.
The drift of a moment
through this moment.
Mysticals merge in the experience,
as they must, or be lost to the absence.

A Room of One's Own

Sometime round December
he'd stopped believing the myth;
patchwork duvet, excess in the pictures,
drapes that struggled
to justify the ever climbing sunflowers,
he now saw as erogenous clutter
to be questioned and purged.

He marked a window
in the north wall,
so he could commune
with the crows,
studied the paint stores
till he lit on a tone
beyond black, that shadowed
discord in the blankets,
the vacant picture frame.

In the clarity of now
the dim world
had a tale to tell,
discreet, if the truth be told.

Constable in Kilkenny

In the lacuna
of a moment
things matter

that I can see
trailer tractor framed
blue in the Mayflowering
careless gap in the hedge.

The precise rays rise
a statement
above substance
trace and track.

Vapours
take shape
In the firmament.

Being Seen through Carroll's Quarries

Even if it's a panorama of ide-
as light and shade
being undone,
a denial, in increments,
of belief that makes you covet
the impossible stability of December days
and moonless nights,
illusions never so ghostly;

though the grasp of the senses
will haul you towards the actual,
a vision of grandeur
in the black and grey
of the carrion crow,
the real, if only you knew it,
invites.
Describable
the way nothing is.

The Oracle Speaks Up

They call me the Oracle of Delphi
and I go along with it,
it gives me power over men.
Alexander, the greatest of them
knelt at my feet .

How I fool politicians,
and poets who write
as if I were something mystical.
I have misled mortals.
I showed them,
when I should have told them.
Mortals love metaphors.

I need to explain that Zeus is not a God,
I am flesh from the future.
It is not possible.
I see millennia of misread myths
that shape the mien, lie on the mind.

Nothing to be Done
After reading Sylvia Plath's ' Lady Lazarus'.

If I could lay you out
on a lenient couch
and softly correct
your contradictions,
heard and unspoken
heart and enchanted,
with my embalmer's hands;

If I were to rid you
of your fiends,
to leave you to
the flesh and blood
of the bread and circuses
you loathe,

If I were to dead head
the hot angst
that burns the grip
of your gossamer traps,
and leave you
silent as a moth in winter,

would you, crushed,
perish in the void,
and leave us,
nothing,
not even a word?

The Free Word

You, the command of the aura
the inescapable call,
the contra–
diction that would
neither nest nor fly
nor be tamed,

word that can't name,

make me want to lavish,
to relish again and cherish
sin and things passed
that, out of reach
repel,
to deny, despite what's evident,
you and I and a void.
To be free, not as a bird.

After John Ashbery's 'The Absence of a Noble Presence'

All that begins
the fires and floods,
the insubstantial strata
of thought and tapestries,
the inconsequential imagined

the voice trained
to lilt and verse,
to beat to sense
my senselessness

is you
who feel
the joy of loss
the grief of love,

not I, not all.
I all words, only, you say.
I catatonic, can not say.

In Spite of What is Known

A wave
could be light
could be love,
rippled the underlay
of the vacant street.

An out of time bell
peeled across
the moonless night.

The wonder of an incident
that's beyond Alpha,
above evidence.

The sacred secret of the divine
revealed
in the hand raised.

I stumbled from the present
toward the undulant tier.

It Can't be a Dolphin – Surely?

A coven of poets has convened
in the lounge of the Livermeed Cliff hotel,
They paint their notions of stasis,
in hypothesis, onto a faint point, all at sea.

Torbay, philosophical today,
waves across a bowed brow,
curved and seasmooth as a cetacean,
the focal point of the party's gaze.

A salty seafaring type
sits unnoticed, back to the wall,
his wish, that he could light his pipe
and sips the froth off his Tetley's ale.

'I would dare compare it to the Yeatsian stone
mute but for the marvel of movement',
murmurs the bearded Guardian reader.
The group is charmed to a sentient quiet.

'I am struck by the symbolism',
ventures the West Country poet with the bossy wife,
'the raised mound suggests defiance,
impertinence to the lapping waves...'

Science distorts the beauty of the stars
as seen through the senses.
One poet longs to view it through the mirror
of the other, 'spatially and temporally'
to tear the rock from the assurance of the concrete,
imagine a magic beyond the prism of perception.

Wit can shake the sanities, release the rapt
to an elsewhere beyond there and here,
from the poisons and potions that condemn the mind

to a worse hex.
So it is with poets
who struggle to affirm the actual
in words writ on water.

The solitary helmsman
who knows it to be a dolphin,
irked by bards who ponder a mirage,
wants to scream look! Look!
such is his rage,
assumes the stance of Saint John the Divine.
in Caravaggio's 'The Taking of Christ'.

Assumpta

You were in your element
the first time I laid eyes on you,
as you helped Mrs Dermody
spruce up her sitting room

you dished out know how
stepping back and forward, hands on hips,
across the improvised kitchen table,

measuring up the wallpaper
cutting it to precision
matching it, even into the corners
where the nosey might
hope to find a flaw.

I wasn't drawn to the design,
if the paper had a design at all,
didn't care if the paint had a silk finish,

I just remember you poised in the elements
focusing on how it could turn out,
wondering if you'd fall;
that your eyes were a special blue
and thinking you were too busy
to notice me.

When This has Passed
For Assumpta

Some day when the beech glistens
of her own accord
and birds take time out,
when bees put buzzing on hold,

we'll share a cryptic coffee
on the ethereal seat
under the willow where
I used to rest.

You will know
if a tingle glides
along your eyes
and a soft breeze
caresses your lips.

Snowdrop

And then,
after the last descent into alcohol
I'll go to your door,
shuffle down the step stones, your design,
through the beds where in summer
Arum Lilies and Gladioli disguise
the dun earth
and for the bleak days, leave,
on your doorstep,
snowdrops, gathered that morning,
moist with dew.

Meeting the Poet
For P.D.

Not a chariot of fire
that could amble on the elemental,
rather, in its stead,
a horse powered car
that lost its cool with the elements
in Rathcoole,
spirited you, eventually,

to Preston House
where we would meet,

not in that mist on Mount Olympus
known to every poet,
but upstairs, in the ethers of Abbeyleix.

'What year is it', you asked,
as you signed my copy of your book ?
Had we, in that Zeus moment,
eclipsed the worldly whims
of space, ink and time ?

Afterwards
I winged it downward
till I made landfall
among the pitfalls
and the charms of the chatty.
How- I know not ?
Recall is a practice
experienced in the Cosmos.

Next day my car was round
the back,
parked and safely home.
There too was your book.
You had written ' magical ' on the fly leaf
among words, raised on the embers
Of Prometheus' present,
That hailed the future.

Passing the Avonmore Plant After a Paul Durcan Reading

Luminous alumina
illuminating
the Ballyragget night.

Little men, dressed in white,
loading the hull
of the Avonmore space oddity
with verbs and adjectives
and strapping casks of oxygen
to the backs
of animate nouns.

The Minister for Agriculture's Penis Speaks Out

"It's going to be a belt and braces job".
- An Irish Minister for Agriculture .

Being my minister's penis
can be a hard job.
My duties are manifold.
When he unfurls the flag
at the G.P.O.
I unfurl in his y-fronts.
I furl in his fur
when he mourns the patriot dead.
When the going gets tuft
and I get tossed
I take refuge
in his windy arbour.

I stand to attention
when he opens
an artificial insemination station.

I am his gossip column
I cover myself with his titbits
titty-bitty-bang-bang-gang-bang
wang-dang-doodle.

My minister has fancy pals,
sometimes he kisses their arse
sometimes they kiss his arse
sometimes I kiss his arse.

The cabinet table is all polish and spittle
because my minister won't change his mind
or his y-fronts,
I know my way round, sometimes
I escape at meetings and see
my friend the Minister for Justice penis.

He's got a stiff neck and a red head and hates blacks
I call him big proud Johnny.
Proud Mary the minister for gas and baths
keeps her penis in the dark.
We can't remember seeing it
it's said she brings it for walks in the park.

Sometimes I stand in for my Minister
during Dáil debates.
I love the manly thrusts with my opposite member
citizen ho-ho-ho-ho-co-co- Kane.
He sniffs around me tries to find
my minister's holes.
I smell like a skunk.
He wears mink willie-warmers
but we've got our holes
with big fat farmers.

I Saw the Minister for Agriculture French kissing

the French Ambassador
as he pinned
the medal of the legion of hon-
our on him;

his frothy tongue
firm as a farm
as he pro-
bed the sur-
prised.

After 'Instruments' on the James Fintan Lalor Avenue, Portlaoise
A sculptural group by Mary McGinty.

Gassed by exhaust fumes,
drowned in the screech
of an ambulance siren
the dismembered, entangled
among the death tools
and weapons of war,
create a language
that speaks across the abyss
to the silenced and blinded.

Beyond the picture
beneath Subway and the Credit Union,
maybe in the cruellest night,
a sickled moon will escape the cloud cover
to reflect, in the unnerved past
of a dishonoured battlefield,
the distorted corpse of a young man
marched to war.

Because art is, above all,
in a glorious moment.
The unheroic will be remembered.

Dei Haven't Gone Away you Know
(On changing the name of Trinity College Dublin)

We were cloistered
in a world of table tennis
and church fetes,
the talk of gossipy women
and agriculture and buns
they now call cupcakes.

We spoke, among ourselves,
our own, lived in language.
We would have read
the name in 'The Irish Times',
or someone would have known
someone who did
divinity in Trinity.

Now we watch, powerless,
in this our colonial present,
(this poem is about us)
as words that distinguish
our quiet difference,
the sap of our lives'
comings and goings,
are slyly rooted out of the mix.

Mary Tudor's Maryboro', battered
to the pancake flat Portlaoise,
is hard to stomach.

And so it goes ,
the power to change names
can change minds,
the needy neoterist
will toil for the day's fix.

Language robbed of its leaven
will speak the indifferent ardour
of the man who has never loved.

The believer, sustained on the crumbs
that warm body and soul, will dare
mumble 'Queencake,' the word
that cannot be kidnapped.

On the Dublin to Belfast Train

Pilgrims of sorts we advanced on Belfast
with options to pass Portadown and its Bannside,
I thought him from Cork such was his accent.
I was on the wrong track; he could have stepped
straight from Samaria such was the pong
off the Brut that he'd bathed in.
He was out for the day this man on a mission.
Lying back I took a discreet position
roundabout midway from Swords to the dark Mournes.

You could say he was an out of sync spiv,
maybe his Dobell waistcoat, sunset orange
sent out a message his pants - faded beige -
could only whisper. The herringbone tweed jacket,
could have been Magee, made it all sound fishy.
Gee he could have been an ageing rocker
on day release from the Betty Ford clinic.

I sensed him close in on the butty pilgrim
in the serge suit with the birthmark on his arse
and Garvaghy a rude word, preaching at him
and half the carriage the news of his forgiving
God, all beads and sandals to his oxters
in the Jordan river.
I thinking Fethard-on-Sea and
battered Jean McConville, buried in sand
the grizzly stirrings laid bare on the beach
those who want will see as the tide retreats.

'And let me ask you', twoshoes went on,
'is your's a forgiving or a forgetting God?
He kept up the needling, I got to hate the prick.
Portydown didn't want to get down and dirty
or talk about churches or marches or young Rosie McCann,
or much else. 'There's bould boyos there you know'
he ventured under pressure. 'Indeed there are
bould boyos', Corky was lording his sayso
driving his point home; the bastard wanted
to shout 'planter' but knew he didn't have to.

I watched wee Porty limp off the platform,
braces hard on his backbone, not a man to bend,
the severed head of his God on a platter
in his outstretched hands, staunched for the siege
to come. The tame train slunk from the station,
Corky at full throttle delivering his homily
'if they would only listen to reason'
(they'd be saved from eternal damnation)

and went on to read the FT. index
writ on the screen of an IPhone the Word
from the bourses Belshazzar reeling
portents of woe from his God in the cloud,
ranted rich bout the bankers and how
If he had his way he would shoot all of them.

By this time Stiffy was snug in his armchair
the 'Belfast Newsletter' spread before him,
the text for the day, better read than dead,
a pack of fags, a mug and a teapot.
Corky a memory, well out of earshot.

•

In Commemoration of the One Hundred and Fifth Anniversary of Joseph Mary Plunkett's Victory in the Algerian Roller Skating Championships, 1911

In this year of memory we query
the champ who roller-skated to glory
in the dusty grit of distant Algeria.

Skaters of fame, though born to the stirrup
may be nurtured by myth round the fireside,
passions hot from past deeds cultural –
a prize set of skates, glammed up and gleaming
hanging in pride from crooks in the ceiling –
drive a man to be star of the era.

With Plunkett JM. 'twas bred in the bone
a sweet body conceived for a mission
explodes 'cross rinks to the whirr of the quad,
buzz of the toe-stop, will to be top dog.

Algeria was Plunkett's nation of choice
weather was good though the sand didn't help
his skating or damned tuberculosis.
dear was the lexis spoke by those tribesmen,
that he studied each day before practise –
Arabic. Their old tongue, long lapsed, is Amazighte.

Did he write poems 'bout inline skating
aggressive or not; or know the Kingbolt
was coming ? Did he pen 'I see his blood
upon the road' for a smashed pal victim
of combative collision, or dream it ?

Laugh you at home in crazes of history
Plunkett's gift, august in North Africa –
no act of deceit to insular Ireland –
the skater hailed in song and in mosque,
others failed holily, his stands remembered –
is loved by skaters throughout Algeria.

Revision

This is how it'll begin:
A snapshot in a Teutonic tabloid,
Viennese maybe,
a forgotten street league final,
the goalie at full stretch
snatches the ball off the boot
of the inrushing striker.

A few weeks later in 'The Guardian'
Weekend – review,
he's in summery casuals,
having the crack
with a few art conscious pals.

The tortured artist
will be reappraised
by a panel of vorticists
on Radio 4.
Still lives, newly unearthed
in a Jewish collector's horde,
it will be said,
concentrate awareness
on his *avant garde* verve.

You know he banned
the boiling of live lobsters?
When word of the act of kindness
makes the cookery columns
of better type magazines
Dublin 4 Adolfins,
such will be their outrage,
will threaten closures
in the seafood sector.

Evidence of escaping gas
will debunk the myth of the camps.
The truth is his orders had them built,
it will be claimed,
to save you from angry investors.

Then we'll get to see the wedding photos.
Exclusives in 'Hello' will hug
the popcultcon with headlines
like 'Adolf and Eva's dreams for a better world'
and " 'I want two children
and an electric grill'
demands the radiant bride."

The world will warm to the couple.
Will the abyss return your gaze?
Who, O Lord, will save your people?

We Too Have our Martyrs

We have reduced the grand narratives –
to our elder's irritation–
passed to us from Israel and Greece,
to an *a la carte* way of doing
that frees us to delight in
a meal with friends, a rock concert,
or a football game.

We elect our rulers.
When they betray our expectations
we exercise our right to censure them in a free press,
If we feel the urge to torture
we express our feelings through satire.

From time to time
the tediously intense among us
believe they can correct
the defects in our system.
We smile and shake our heads, knowingly.
Our ways accommodate such vagaries.
We call them Western Values.

Our menus and match programmes
are as sacred to us
as your scriptures are to you.
Though we do not feel the need to sing it
from the rooftops
we too, the people, are believers.

You who grieve for your martyrs of long ago,
you of a heightened sense of your persecution
carried down the ages,
best be aware
of who you are taking on.
We are not the pampered, guilt ridden liberals,
you suppose us to be,
soft targets on a night out
in the decadent West.
We too can match hurt for hurt.
We too have our martyrs,
those who died by your hand
not in the heat of battle,
but in the savagery of cold blooded slaughter.

They inspire us.
Our hearts bleed with their hearts.
They died because of what we are,
their beliefs live in us.

'To the Water's Edge'
Oliver and Liat Shurmann's Garden

A rare event is remembered
the colonnades, maybe things filtered
through layers
and presented passion less.

The greenery has long turned
its back
on the desire to deceive.

We think a new reality
beyond representation,
air and water

table and chairs.
So perceived
the saddest wonder.

Art Thou Not Also One of His Disciples?
After 'Saint Peter Denying Christ'

(Pensionante del Sareceni)

Salvation Army jacket frayed,
shoulder thread bare,
a few follicles resisting
the high lights.
The fabric that held
his body together ravels.
She rips through him,
as devout disciples do
in times of spin.

'You stitched him up
with your "I know not the man,"
not even a hello out of you. '

The crafted sermons,
the indulgent rage in the porch,
the ego trip on the lough,

the matrix looms
over him
in the preternatural night.

In time – after Emmaus,
the ghostly fibre, the hologram –
He would understand
The necessity for yarns,
the mohair shawl of the masses,
and could say,
He is not the man I know or am.

If We Were to Think About It
After Edward Hopper's 'Hotel Room'

Things unimaginable
sensed in your paintings
confront our dreamy notion of reality.

Reduced to basics
the imagined is a pretty
dull state of affairs
hardly worth the bother
if we were to think about it.

Clutter in the corner,
the labelled suitcase
packed and ready to go
no longer suits.
Defined borders
stark shapes
leave nothing
to be desired.

We think she
is reading,
her face a silhouette.
The eye sees what
we cannot see;
bare walls
blank page
the clarity of the magnified absence.

Can it matter?

Body and soul akimbo
beyond caring
connecting to the obvious.

Fazed

It may have been in his blue phase,
in the way that things make sense
to us eventually,
the white-skimmed cones that he
later called peaks
were high enough to be trivial,
that he pondered the absence
of detail,
the formlessness of the chora.

All this matters, he thought,
as he gazed at the blue haze,
from these beginnings.

It was then he saw the light
it may have been sun
taking issue
defining the mountain top
scrubbed and shaping
a reality that made him
feel at home.

Barry's Blind
After a video by Barry Doyle

To wake to broken lines
within a broad rectangle
the unimaged that spells
the day to come,
the mirage that promises
shapes and symmetry,
sums and stories,

haunts
those willow leaves
that waltz in the astral winds,
whimsical, withdrawn.

Barry's drawn Venetian is blind
to the shadowy sirens.
They make light of its lexical design
and the earth's gravitational pull.

Their day-defying dance sways
to music unplayed,
an imprint marked out.

In the Beginning Was...
After 'Market Day, Finistere, 1882'
Henry Jones Thaddeus, National Gallery of Ireland

Though not born of the sea
the eerie sea prepared them.
Its currents and Westerlies,
its spring tides and reflected moons,
stirred in them the promise of reality
and the notion of hunger.

Washed up on the steady sand
and acting on impulse and memory
they trade food on primal stalls
and dream of sex.
Their vision is of an in land,
a gigantic illusion conceived
on this infertile shore.

This lush earth-maid values
the five firm leeks lying
in wait in her wicker egg womb
and will not share them
with the plaintiff waif in the blue beret
who will paint the pain in bedsits
In Stockholm and Copenhagen.

So it is – not a cause – a possibility.
The weathered Oracle's flinty gaze communes
with the chalked calm –
beyond the oceanic roar –
that is in her, and in us all.
She approves.

Though she knows those hips
will people the barren earth,
that their stock will create
mathematics and Morris Dancing,
nuclear power and mythology,
she also knows
that taking the chance to explore
love and hurt
is part of the experiment
that must be seen through.

The Servant Girl and her Other
After 'The Kitchen Window'
Leo Whelan, Crawford Art Gallery, Cork.

I am not the girl
who spits on the silver urn,
my hands, out of habit, polish;
who watches paint peel
from a cupboard door
that struggles for symmetry
with the clutter of the chequered curtain.

Nor am I she
who has gazed too often
through the tyrannous window,
barred and sashed,
on hungry men traipsing,
in solemn line,
across a sunlit yard.

She is the drudge dreary me
who cannot see that I, the girl who speaks
through silence and polka dots,
looks out of the picture,
beyond the gleam in the spot
on the horizon.

While Joseph was Napping on his Trusty Crutch...
After a painting of the Holy Family

I didn't mean to do it,
I was watching her hands
poised over me, wondering
what she would do with them,
waving my arms about,
as all babies do,
aimlessly, maybe hoping
to find something to grip,
or put in my mouth.

I didn't know he was asleep,
that the clamour was the sound
of one human being snoring,
when I felt it in my hand,
something round and smooth
and lovely to touch.

Well, I wanted to chew on it,
that's what babies like, isn't it ?
So I pulled it towards me
with an almighty heave.

Oh God! All hell broke loose;
He crashed down, just missing me,
banging his head off the floor.
She grabbed me and pulled me close
babbling and crying and shouting at him
'you could have killed him, you stupid man,
you could have killed my begotten son'.

The New Covenant

Lured by the rumour of something seen
the heart seems to pause in defiance.
What it is – no real matter?
In this moment a force affirms
the triumph of fist pricked furze
or fox cubs between April showers,
of Venus and November

over the hushed voice
of the here and now,
etherized
unseen and unknown,
the leavened bread from which
all things are made.

Take this and eat.

Sometimes you Have to Say It

because there's a notion in you
that hates the silence
that succeeds the diktat
and you feel good about
the defined outrage.

In the composure of the moment
you, the hero of the hour,
capture the words,
precisely.

And I who cannot feel or think,
or say this or that,
distance myself from the violence
because that is not it.

"Poetry is like bread, it should be shared by all, by scholars and by peasants, by all our vast, incredible, extraordinary family of humanity."

- Pablo Neruda

Revival Press is a community publishing press and is the poetry imprint of The Limerick Writers' Centre. It was founded by managing editor Dominic Taylor in 2007. It grew out of the Revival Poetry Readings established in Limerick 2003 by Barney Sheehan and Dominic Taylor. It has published over thirty poetry titles to date plus three anthologies including *I Live in Michael Hartnett*, an anthology of poems written to celebrate the life and work of the late County Limerick poet. Revival has also helped establish a number of local and national poets by publishing their first collections.

One of the aims of Revival Press is to make writing and publishing both available and accessible to all. It tries as much as possible to represent diverse voices and advocates for increased writing and publishing access to individuals and groups that have not typically had this access.
It continues to represent local authors and to offer advice and encouragement to aspiring writers.

Revival Press supports Fair Trade Publishing.